CANALETTO

ABOUT THE AUTHOR

Dr. Giuseppe M. Pilo is Director of the Museum in
Bassano del Grappa, Italy.

DR. GIUSEPPE M. PILO

Canaletto

BLANDFORD PRESS
LONDON

editor: Anthony Bosman
lay-out: Wim van Stek
First published in the English edition in 1962
by Blandford Press Ltd London
Reprinted 1968
© 1962 and printed in Holland by The Ysel Press Ltd., Deventer

'Whatever he paints—whether it is buildings, water, clouds or images, he gives an impression of vitality, so that the objects are shown in their most imposing light. He makes use of some artistic licence, but with moderation, so that the ordinary viewer can find Nature in his works, and the connoisseur Art. In this he excels'.

Thus did Lanzi describe Canaletto's paintings, clarifying once and for all the misunderstanding that his view was a faithful imitation of reality, as insinuated by Guarienti (in 1753), when the artist was still alive, in speaking of a 'deception of the eye'. On the other hand Antonio Maria Zanetti (1771) wrote enthusiastic words about Canaletto praising his 'beautiful neat colours and exquisite effortless touches of the brush, the work of a serene mind and a happy genius'. Already in 1736 Count Tessin unhesitatingly declared him to be the leading Venetian painter of his time; and De Brosses also stated that, in his view, 'il surpasse tout ce qu'il y a jamais eu', adding that 'sa manière est claire, gaie, vive, perspective et d'un détail admirable' (1739-40).

And yet it was by his supposed 'imitation of reality' that Canaletto gained his reputation in the academic circles of the nineteenth century, although even then a real and intelligent understanding of his art was shown by people like Sagredo and Blanc; this was followed by a widespread unfavourable criticism in our century that for a long time dismissed him as a second class painter, carried away as it was by the enthusiasm arising from the re-discovery of

Francesco Guardi and the atmosphere of new perceptions created by the Impressionists.

Meanwhile, Canaletto's true nature was being brought to light by the research of Finberg who was reconstructing the artist's English period; by Von Hadeln, who dedicated one book to his drawings; by Fritsche, Pittaluga and Pallucchini who, through the study of his water-colours, gave a more convincing interpretation of Canaletto. There followed the monographs of Watson and Moschini, the discerning studies of Longhi and Ragghianti, and a new evaluation of his drawings by Parker, Moschini and Pignatti. Whilst awaiting the great work on Canaletto promised by W. G. Constable, some very good essays by A. Pallucchini, Brandi and Valcanover were published. A very neat profile of the artist has been published now by Rodolfo Pallucchini in his history of 'Venetian Painting of the Eighteenth Century' where, availing himself of his experience of University teaching, he gives us objectively the most enlightened and up to date picture of Canaletto in relation to the century in which he lived and to contemporary opinion.

Giovanni Antonio Canal, called Canaletto, was born in Venice on the 18th of October 1697. When he was twenty he started working as scene-painter with his father, who taught him this art, and his brother Cristoforo. Between 1716 and 1718 he worked with them for the theatres of Sant'Angelo and San Cassiano on the scenes of some operas, among them 'Arsilda regina di Ponto' and 'Incoronazione di Dario' by Antonio Vivaldi. These were 'serious operas' and they gave him the chance—we do not know how important this was—to meet the 'Red Priest' (Vivaldi) and also, whilst he was still very young, to use huge and complicated theatrical machinery for the traditional baroque scenery which was required. Such experience certainly influenced the artist and supplied him with

6

ideas for perspective that are easily recognisable in his early paintings.

But Canaletto's theatrical apprenticeship did not last long. The historians of the time inform us that, having become impatient with the theatrical world, 'he solemnly excommunicated the theatre' — to quote Zanetti — and decided to change his artistic activities and also his surroundings. As a result of this artistic crisis, he moved to Rome in 1719 and dedicated himself to painting landscapes. There he must have been impressed not so much by the great architecture and the allegorical paintings of the Roman baroque, which he had already repudiated in his heart, as by works depicting nature in its reality and true scenes of humble every-day life, such as the small pictures — despised by the official critics of the time — by the Dutch painters that had come to Rome the previous century. In his day, also, there were artists who painted scenes of quiet and humble village life; for instance the small and true-to-life small paintings of Gaspar Van Wittel who, according to Mariette, probably influenced the vision of the young Canaletto in those early years. It was probably in Rome that he first experimented in landscapes. We do not know how he started painting in Rome, as nothing is left of his works in those first two years. In 1720 he returned to Venice where it is recorded he joined the Painters' Association.

One of his first works in Venice is certainly the 'Piazza di San Marco' (St. Mark's Square) (p. 20) which used to belong to the Liechtenstein collection and is now included in the collection of Baron Van Thyssen of Lugano; this must have been painted before 1723 (Pallucchini) because the new paving of the square by Andrea Tirali, which was completed in that year, is not shown in the painting. The setting of the background shows the influence of Carlevaris, in fact G. A. Moschini states that Canaletto was a pupil of Carlevaris. Perhaps Carlevaris, who was the founder of the Venetian school of the eighteenth century, was not actually his tutor, but his influence is evident here. The size of the square and its perspective are intentionally altered and the wings of the Doges' Palace are extended so as to create an illusion of greater spaciousness. One can visualize the gust of wind carrying the clouds in the sky and tossing the multi-coloured tents of the stalls in front of the basilica and at the foot of St. Mark's bell-tower. This is already a long way from the still air of Carlevaris, in whose skies the clouds themselves stressed the perspective aspect of the image represented. In contrast with the shadow, in which the portals of the basilica are submerged, the size of the square is greatly amplified by the rather high line of the horizon and is crowded with small bright spots drawn with heavy, full strokes of the brush which vividly brings Carlevaris to mind.

During this first phase Canaletto seems to combine the severity of perspective painting with his own interpretation of the view, which is not strictly faithful to reality, but turned into poetry. This is the case also in other paintings of the Liechtenstein collection: the 'Rio dei Mendicanti' which belongs to the same period of 'Piazza S. Marco' and two views of the Grand Canal of a slightly later date: 'da Ca' Foscari verso Rialto' (p. 19) and 'da S. Vio alla Salute', which are now in the collection of Mario Crespi in Milan. In his view of the 'Canal Grande da Ca Foscari a Rialto' Canaletto proves his free approach to the Venetian scenes. The Grand Canal almost takes the form of a funnel, so that in the reflection of the water he can set that unforgettable cargo-boat with the colourful lowered sails, and freely play with chiaroscuro effects in painting the intensely picturesque banks of the Canal in which are reflected the deep and rich colours of the houses. Canaletto seems to prefer the warmest and brightest shades of colours: red, ivory yellow rich brown, in harmony with the row of red brick roofs under

PORTRAIT OF CANALETTO,
engraved by Antonio Visentini after a drawing by
Giambattista Piazzetta.

a stormy, spring sky, covered by thick clouds in a sultry, almost heavy atmosphere. This vibration in the humid air shows how Canaletto in his first works, probably painted between 1723 and 1725, although using a few effects learned from Carlevaris, knows how to add a soulful quality to Carlevaris' often cold and mechanical style.

A masterpiece among Canaletto's paintings in those first years is certainly the large view of the 'Canal Grande a S. Angelo' (Grand Canal at St. Angelo) (p. 22). A close arrangement of perspective lines brings to light the complex and imposing outline of this memorable view with the delightful group of cargo-boats in the foreground and the view rising superbly up to the Rialto bridge. Between the vast sky covered with heavy clouds and the water cut by the reflection of the palaces, the air seems to become magically tinted and there is a daring feeling of true perspective that forestalls the arduous and romantic conquest of the atmosphere that Francesco Guardi was to attempt quarter of a century later, taking his artistic inspiration from these first works of Canaletto. Perhaps just because they loved the light touch and the atmosphere of Guardi's paintings, the critics of our century confined their appreciation, for many decades, to Canaletto's early works, denying an objective valuation to his works of the English period and of his mature years, which to-day we consider just as good. On the other hand, it cannot be denied that Canaletto produced some masterpieces in those early years.

Between 1725 and 1726 Canaletto painted for Stefano Conti of Lucca four pictures which are now in Montreal in the Pillow collection, which show four stately views of Venice: 'Ponte di Rialto col Palazzo dei Camerlenghi', 'Canal Grande con le Fabbriche nuove', painted between August and November 1725, 'Canal Grande con la Chiesa della Carità' (p. 26) and 'Campo di SS. Giovanni e Paolo'. The sketch for the 'Ponte di

Rialto' (Rialto Bridge) (p. 32) is kept in the Ashmolean Museum of Oxford. In the Oxford drawing the chiaroscuro contrast is indicated merely with a few lines; moreover a few notes on it reveal the method already followed in his works by Canaletto in those early years and his particular feeling about the at-mospherical phenomenon as poetic inspiration. The word 'sun' which is written on the sun-drenched part of the Grand Canal, contrasting with the shadowy part, in this sketch, shows us that the factor of light was for Canaletto an authentic con-structive element of the view. The exceptional light that covers the lower arch of the Rialto and the façade of the Fondaco dei Tedeschi against a thick stormy sky is certainly an exaggerated image of Canaletto's fantasy and he seems to catch it at a particular time of a summer day; it becomes the prevailing feature of the picture. This is actually the predominant medium of expression of his poetic imagination and, if we learn to recognize it in its different aspects, we can follow the develop-ment, through the years, of Canaletto's interpretation of the views he painted.

The treatment of light and shade, which was favoured by Canaletto in his early years, seems to be the salient feature of his paintings around 1725. This is proved by the view of the 'Canal Grande con la Chiesa della Carità', which is one of the paintings now in Montreal, where the shadow of the ancient church of la Carità, with its spires, projected onto the façade of the church, in contrast with the warm afternoon light, creates an intense and dramatic chiaroscuro effect. This effect is accentuated in the part of the bridge that stands out in the glaring light in the foreground, and it seems to come forward towards the viewer so that he participates in the painted scene. This same effect, enhanced by Canaletto's vivid fantasy, is also evident in the stupendous view of 'Isole di S. Cristoforo della pace e S. Michele verso Murano' (p. 28) which is now in the Royal

Collection at Windsor Castle. As in other paintings, where he shows monuments of his city, in this scene of a lesser-known part of Venice Canaletto feels deeply the poetry of the Lagoon and its subtle qualities of atmosphere and light, shown in the subdued shades of red and in the deep blue of the humid sky covered by clouds slowly carried by the sultry wind, whilst stillness and quietness reigns over the distant waters of the Lagoon.

This intense and almost moving chiaroscuro effect is also seen in the six vertical views of the Square of St. Mark and its surroundings painted for Joseph Smith—who was later to become British Consul in Venice. These are also kept in the Royal Collection of Windsor Castle and they are probably dated between 1726 and 1727 (Watson). In the picture 'Piazzetta verso S. Giorgio Maggiore' (p. 39), for example, the corner of the Doges' Palace exposed to the pale sun contrasts with the dark, enlarged outline of the isle of St. George, whilst a ray of light breaks through the stormy and sultry sky creating a daring, almost romantic atmosphere.

Canaletto's imagination is greatly impressed by the play of light and shade effects on the monuments and buildings of Venice which produce almost an effect of decadence. Apart from the drawings (p. 38) of the Square and of its surroundings, this is also found in the picture of 'Chiesa della Carità da S. Vitale' (Church of La Carità from St. Vitale or The Stonemason's Yard) (p. 34), in the National Gallery in London, which is probably the masterpiece among Canaletto's early works. It is extraordinary how Canaletto in this has caught the poetic details of the material things represented: the red brick colour of the Church of la Carità and of the bell tower which collapsed in 1744, the red, pink and greyish colours of the humble houses most of which no longer exist to-day, the stall of the stone-cutter with his marble; all these true details are

12

used and transfigured by Canaletto with the chiaroscuro treatment which perhaps is never as intense and touching as here, reminding us of the rich and vigorous colours and chiaroscuro effect of Giambattista Piazzetta.

It was then, in the middle thirties of the eighteenth century, that the romantic chiaroscuro technique introduced by Giambattista Piazzetta and by Federico Bencovich, in direct contrast with the rococo that had been the rage in Venice for about thirty years, became a style of painting of powerful dramatic contrasts of colour and light, with the right juxtaposition of light and shade. This was actually the style that Gian Battista Tiepolo chose for his first experiments, joining Piazzetta and Bencovich in their daring movement which was the renewal in the eighteenth century of that chiaroscuro treatment that had been the prevailing feature in the paintings of the seventeenth century in Italy and Holland. Rodolfo Pallucchini was the first to realize that Canaletto was influenced, in his early years, by the dramatic style of Piazzetta and Bencovich and of the young Tiepolo; we can now understand the first artistic phase of Canaletto which is in complete contrast with his later works. A contrast there certainly was. A fact that also contributed to his change of style was the commission which he received from Owen McSwiny for the two allegoric 'Tombs' in memory of Lord Somers, which are now in Birmingham in the Plymouth collection; in these Canaletto takes from Marco Ricco for the ruins, from Piazzetta for the figures, and from Cimaroli for the landscape. And so through his connection with Smith and McSwiny began Canaletto's association with England, where the artist paid several long visits and where many of his works went.

It was McSwiny, a business man who had been a theatrical impresario and then became a buyer of pictures for English art collectors, who commissioned him in 1727 to do two land-

13

scapes on copper for the Duke of Richmond: the 'Rialto Bridge' and 'Canal Grande con le Fabbriche Nuove', two themes that had already been chosen two years earlier for Stefano Conti. It is clear that Canaletto's feeling about light effects has changed. Here also the lower arch of the Rialto bridge is illuminated, but it dominates the scene with a more compact and uniform brightness and there is a wealth of detail never used before. Canaletto, in other words, was starting to take an objective view of things instead of concentrating, as he had done so far, in the thematic treatment of light and shadow. This was in 1727; and it is Pallucchini again who tells us that in the same year Giovan Battista Tiepolo, in his frescoes for the Archbishop of Udine, had resisted following the romantic chiaroscuro tendency of the Venetian school and had instead concentrated on the study of light effects.

Evidently Canaletto was following the same course taken by this great artist, who was his contemporary. Although their choice of subject and their perception of reality in the century in which they lived was very different, from then on they adopted the same style.

I think that the splendid 'Veduta del Dolo' (View of Dolo on the Brenta Canal) (p. 40), now in the Ashmolean Museum at Oxford, belongs to this happy moment of his artistic career, in which he shows a renewed feeling of light and colour. Here for the first time Canaletto breaks off from his favourite themes centred around the Lagoon of Venice to explore, as he did from then on, the Venetian country and, in particular, the shores of the Brenta which were so loved by the society of his time. In the bright and serene air the soft spring shades of the pink and blue dresses of the ladies have the natural beauty of flowers blooming in the fresh morning air.

What effect of fantastic splendour can be achieved with this interpretation of light can be seen in the two magnificent

14

canvases in the Aldo Crespi's collection in Milan: 'Ricevimento dell'ambasciatore imperiale conte Bolagno' (Reception of the Imperial Ambassador Count Bolagno) (p. 25) painted in 1729 and 'Festa dell' Ascensione' (Festival of the Ascension) (p. 24) which were a turning point in Canaletto's artistic activity during those years. In the view 'Ricevimento del Bolagno' the gala procession of the barges, the Doges and the dignitaries proceeding towards the Ducal Palace from the Molo, against the superb background of the Library and the Customs Building with the Basilica della Salute, creates a phantasmagoria of extremely vivid colours, with a new and gay brightness that is found again in the 'Festa dell'Ascensione' where the mood of the whole crowd is caught by a clever use of colours: the barges around the Bucentaur in the foreground and the delightful detail of the ladies carrying parasols, the oarsmen in shirt sleeves and the crowds gathering on the Molo. In this luminous air, purified by the fresh sea wind, the oarsmen's costumes in all shades of red, blue, green and yellow give an extremely bright effect to the scene and convey perfectly the supreme excitement and gaiety of the festivity of the Venetian Republic, reaching an intensity of colour and light that is only equalled in the great paintings of his contemporary, G.B. Tiepolo. To quote Lanzi 'Canaletto loves to create a grand effect and in this he rather resembles Tiepolo . . .'

There is no doubt that Canaletto can catch the realities of life around him with a very acute eye, showing a deep understanding which was sadly lacking in his times. It is also true that, although Canaletto and Tiepolo differ in their perception of the society of their time and in the choice of themes for their paintings, they have in common this exciting brightness of colours which made them the leading artists of eighteenth century Venice. It has been said that Tiepolo reached this supreme brightness of colours by using the chromatic technique

15

of Paolo Veronese and probably the 'renewed' style of Sebastiano Ricci, one of the founders of the Venetian Rococo, who was also a follower of Paolo Veronese. I do not know to what extent Canaletto may have been influenced by the great works of Paolo Veronese, who reproduced on his canvas Palladio's luminous architecture in a prodigious juxtaposition of colours. But I think that, if he was not influenced by Paolo Veronese, then Canaletto had the same intense feeling about colours that was, of course, somewhat damped by the 'cold realistic air' of his time, whilst Paolo Veronese lived in a paradisaical atmosphere which not even Tiepolo enjoyed. It is obvious that the themes of Canaletto's paintings, which conform closely to those of Paolo Veronese, are not consistent with the mood of his time.

To this period belong the 'Punta della Dogana' and 'Piazzetta col bacino di S. Marco', both in the Mario Crespi's collection in Milan; the 'Canal Grande a S. Vio' in the Brera Gallery (p. 30) and 'Bacino di S. Marco' (The Basin of St. Mark) (p. 33) in the Kunsthistoriches Museum in Vienna. There is no trace any more of the romantic feeling shown in the 'Bacino di S. Marco della Piazzetta' painted around 1726-7, which is in Windsor. In the Vienna picture, painted only four years later, the basin is viewed from the shore of S. Biagio with a very acute optical precision, which has no precedent in Venetian paintings. The same can be said of the 'Bacino di S. Marco e della Salute dal Molo' (St. Mark's Basin and the Church of la Salute from the Molo) (p. 43) which belongs to a private collection and which, I think, has not been exhibited so far, where the buildings, the boats and the people stand out almost too obtrusively in a sun-drenched scene.

It has been suggested that these extremely neat views, in which Canaletto fully realizes his talent, have been influenced by Dutch painters like Van der Heyden (Fiocco), Berckheyde and others. But in the collection of Joseph Smith, which includes many works by Canaletto and which was bought *in toto* by Richard Dalton in 1762 for George III, to become one of the most precious possessions of English Royalty, there was a picture by Vermeer 'The Music Lesson' which Canaletto, who was then already in very good terms with Smith, certainly knew. It was from Vermeer, the only true Nordic interpreter of Caravaggio, that Canaletto got his inspiration when he started painting from Nature as the views that were painted around 1730 show.

This talent of reproducing details with startling reality by means of light effects, for which he deserves to be compared the great Dutch painters of the seventeenth century, is evident in the paintings in which he portrays the most expressive aspects of his city. To the fourth decade of the eighteenth century belong the 38 views of the three series of Venetian monuments, engraved by Visentini and issued in 1742; they comprise 14 views of the first series painted for Smith, now in Windsor, which were followed a few years later by the series for the Duke of Bedford, and then the third series which is in the Harvey collection in Langley Park. If one compares the view of the 'Canal Grande con la Chiesa della Carità' (p. 41), now in Windsor, with the previous views of the same place, one notes that the subdued and romantic use of colours of his early years, showing his dramatic awareness, was followed later by a placid vision, seen in a diffuse and penetrating light. Before Canaletto's acute eyes all the aspects of the Grand Canal from the Church of la Salute to St. Chiara pass by in a fascinating parade, like a valuable documentary, of the marble of large buildings next to the colourful humble houses and the scenes of daily happenings along the Canal, caught as through a telescope in a sensitive and translucent atmosphere. (p. 21, 23, 29, 31)

Now Canaletto's style is attaining maturity and to this period belongs the 'Festa di S. Rocco' (p. 35) of the National Gallery in London, in which the Doges' procession comes to life in the happy sparkle of the bright, vivid colours, drawn with a firm flowing brush that gives character to the faces in the shadow where only the vivacious expression of the eyes is visible and the features are merely touched with a few sensitive and curved lines. The extent to which Canaletto was capable of developing this particular talent of his can be seen by comparing these perfectly drawn details with those which animate the view of the 'Carità da S. Vitale' (p. 37) in the small world of the stone-cutter. This sunny and happy moment of Canaletto's splendid maturity is shown in the portrayal of the traditional sumptuous festivities in Venice, such as the various 'Regatta' pictures which are in the National Gallery in London and in Windsor Castle, and in the 'Ritorno del Bucintoro' (The Old Venetian State Barge) (p. 57), in Mario Crespi's collection in Milan, which offers him the opportunity to portray another superb vision of the Basin of St. Mark in an astonishing wealth of bright colours. There are hints of the chromatic perfection that he achieves here in some of the pictures painted earlier like 'Fonteghetto della Farina' (p. 27), which belongs to the Giustiniani collection in Venice, a golden study of the sun on the yellowish wall in a warm afternoon, caught in one of the most delightful parts of the city in front of the Church of la Salute.

The aspects of everyday life in Venice are also presented with poetic reality in the views of the Bedford (p. 59) and Harvey series. They are mainly 'fields', which were the subject of many pictures of the fourth decade of the eighteenth century. The original sketches of these paintings are in Canaletto's 'Copybook', which was donated in 1949 by Guido Cagnola, a nobleman, to the Gallery in Venice. There are here 138 sketches taken down by Canaletto in a great hurry and often with a

18

(Continued on page 73)

29

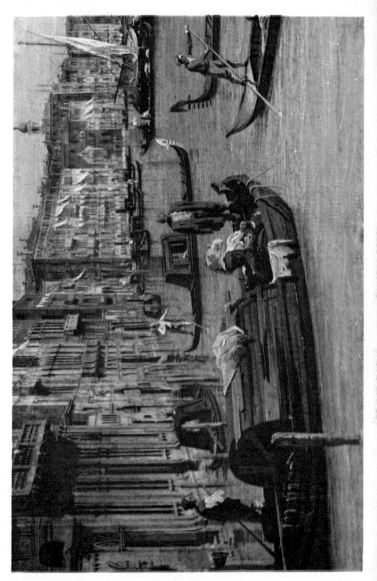

Veduta dal ponte di rialto infaca verbon

32

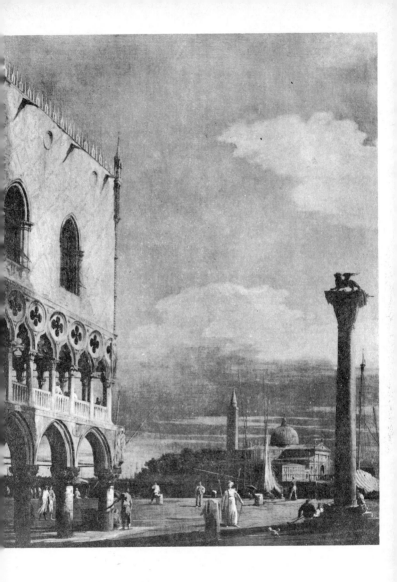

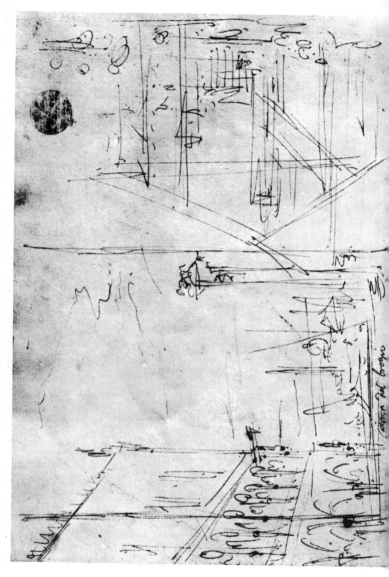

42

43

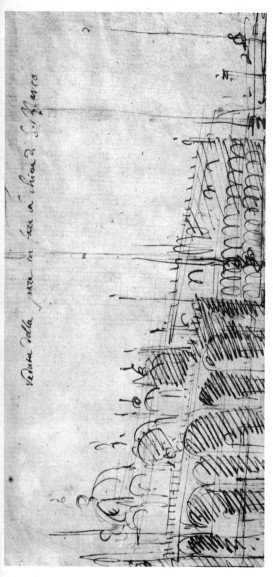

Veduta della piazza in faccia a chiesa di S. Marco

51

54

fresh creative mind; they are actually notes, taken by the artist from life, which he used afterwards as models to develop the painted views. The method followed by Canaletto in his work has been described and argued at length by Moschini, Pignatti and Gioseffi. There is an utterly poetic quality in some of the sketches in the 'Copybook', like those of the 'Piazzetta di S. Marco e il Molo' (p. 42), 'Piazza dalle Procuratie Vecchie' (p. 56), 'Ponte dei tre archi di Cannareggio'; these are very hurriedly outlined sketches which show the keen and inexhaustable curiosity of this quaint 'little man' as Hinchcliffe described him when he met him, years later, when he was painting from Nature. We can imagine him tirelessly going around the squares, the buildings, and the canals of his city to discover every aspect of it and to reproduce on the canvas the walls, the stones, the canals of Venice that was—it has been said—'exclusively his'. Zanetti wrote that the *camera ottica* (a sort of *camera obscura*), which historians assure us he used when he painted, taught Canaletto how to avoid blemishes, especially in the shades, and to eliminate from the view anything that may have offended the aesthetic appearance of the picture. He merely used it as an additional device to confine and bring into smaller compass the scene that had caught his eye and confer unity to it, omitting any irrelevant details. In other words, the *camera ottica* helped Canaletto to bring reality to his views, because he knew how to make it serve his purpose, which was a fanciful interpretation of reality.

And this was always the case. Even in this period, when Canaletto seems more inclined to a faithful and objective style of painting, an 'enlightened reality' as it was suitably defined by Longhi, he still submits real details to his own perception of the view.

At the same time as he painted the Harvey views, such as 'Campo di San Giuseppe con la chiesa di S. Nicolò di Castello'

73

(p. 45), (which is a view of the outskirts of Venice where it borders on the Lagoon, interpreted with a clear 'stereoscopic' perception of the scene, as shown by the poles placed in a line like luminous beacons and by the delightful festive church of S. Nicolò), Canaletto started painting great panoramas, set mainly in the Basin of St. Mark, as for example the views now in the Wallace Collection in London, especially 'dal Piazzale di S. Giorgio Maggiore' (p. 49). Here in the incredibly translucent air which only Canaletto can produce, the domes and the belfries of the city throb in a display of sparkling and deep colours. And they do so also in the views which used to be in Castle Howard, one of which, 'Bacino di S. Marco e l'isola di S. Giorgio' (pp. 47, 55), is now in the Boston Museum.

The cargo-boats in the foreground, the English vessels and the masts scanning the huge space, intentionally enlarged, are untrue to life and yet 'more real than reality' as only a passionate interpretation of reality can be. Because among those shrouds, the carefully measured space between the masts under the high sky covered with light clouds merely outlined, there is a salty atmosphere that can only be compared with the most fanciful impressions, somewhere between reality and dream, of Vittore Carpaccio. Since Carpaccio Venice had never had (nor has it had afterwards) an interpreter as sensitive as Canaletto of the poetry that can be seen any day in the buildings and in the waters of Venice. The vision of the Basin of St. Mark moves before our eyes, in the Boston picture, slowly and solemnly up to the Church of Sant'Elena near the Lido and the open Lagoon. In some of his drawings of that period, now in the Royal Library of Windsor and the Ashmolean Museum in Oxford, he chooses the most exciting landscapes of the Lagoon, such as the view 'Sant'Elena e il Lido' (The Isle of Sant'Elena and the Lido) (p. 46), where with a few light strokes he evokes the still, melancholic light of the flat horizon in a deeply felt and lingering monotony which shows Canaletto's feeling of loneliness. No other artist can catch these fleeting moments of the Venetian scene as Canaletto did (p. 44).

There was in him, side by side with his lucid objectivity and not in contrast with it, a lyrical vein often inclined to romanticism, as shown in his view 'Funzione notturna nella Basilica di S. Marco' now in Windsor.

The light effects, against the deep shade surrounding the vaults and the domes of the basilica, with the luminous drops falling along the Cross and the lamps, are a prelude to his later style, after he came back from his last journey in England – as in the unforgettable light effects on the white arches of the Walton Bridge and in his last views of the St. Mark's Square. But perhaps Canaletto had already started using these effects in 1740. It is a fact that in this period Canaletto showed almost suddenly an inclination to escape from reality and rely more on his imagination. It is likely that, as suggested by Voss, Canaletto made a second trip to Rome which resulted in his five views of the Roman ruins: 'Foro', 'Arco di Settimio Severo', 'Arco di Costantino', 'Pantheon', (p. 60), and 'Arco di Tito', signed and dated 1742, all in Windsor Castle; and then 'Il Colosseo' of Hampton Court dated 1743 and the view of 'Basilica di Massenzio e S. Francesca Romana' belonging to the Campanini-Bonomi collection in Milan. In these we rediscover Canaletto's golden and caressing atmosphere, his feeling for material objects like old stones and bricks and the burnt grass of the soil which had already inspired Marco Ricci and Zais. These are perhaps details taken from his impressions of the Roman ruins, which Canaletto used in his fanciful views in which he associates real details with imaginary images often set in unreal surroundings as in 'Veduta fantastica con S. Francesco della Vigna', belonging to an Italian collection. In one picture he sets the Rialto Bridge (as designed by Palladio) in the Grand Canal; in a view of the

Forum the monument to Colleoni; in the Piazzetta he sets the four horses of St. Mark. With clever light effects he makes these rather strange tricks acceptable and persuasive; '*fantasque e bourru*', is how the Count of Tessin called him in 1736; and McSwiny in 1727 had already described him as eccentric. We find genuine poetry and this lyrical quality of his in his etchings rather than in the pictures painted for Smith. In Venice the time was ripe to appreciate these supreme creations of Canaletto's imagination. In 1730 Venice had seen the twenty etchings of Marco Ricci, which are in the Orsolini collection; the views of Michele Marieschi were published in 1741; and in 1743 the 'Capricci' by G.B. Tiepolo. Canaletto's 34 etchings were made between 1740 and 1744. It was in 1744 that Smith—to whom 31 etchings collected in one volume had been dedicated—became British Consul in Venice. There is no doubt that these are the most intimate and lyrical poetic expressions of the century. Almost 'dreams of a lonely walker', as they were called by A. Pallucchini, they portray real objects together with visions and dreams, united by the medium of light that here more than ever is Canaletto's imaginative means of expression.

'Views, some portrayed from Nature, others imagined' this is how he entitled this peerless series. Here he goes back to the Venetian landscape and, in particular, to the banks of the Brenta, as in 'View of Dolo' (p. 58). What is surprising is the almost elementary simplicity of the means used by Canaletto to reach such supreme results: these views are mainly parallel lines which become thicker only where shadow effects are wanted; he seldom uses intersected lines.

Therefore, the secret of the method that was described by Manet '*souple et charmante*' lies in the exposition and in the mobility of his strokes: curved or marked, or sometimes almost obsessively disarranged as in the field on the right side of the

Io Zuane Antonio da Canal, deto il Canaleto
lò dissegnià è
fatto

RUSTIC HOUSES AND TERRACE
After 1755, pen and brown ink with grey wash, heightened
with little white, 14 x 10 in. Berlin, Kupferstichkabinett

Church of Dolo and at the foot of 'Casa del 1741' (p. 54), where the light is drawn with a few undulating strokes, which remind us of Van Gogh. Elsewhere, as in 'Torre di Malghera' (p. 48) a single block of dazzling light dominates the scene, determining immediately the predominant detail in the view: such as the tower under the burning sun, which is the outstanding feature in the great Lagoon bathed in a subdued, melancholia; and in the 'Portico con lanterna' (p. 53) that poor nameless house which attracts the viewer's attention immediately. Sometimes in the portrayal of hilly landscapes Canaletto reminds us of Marco Ricci, whose influence is always felt in the style. But is it clear, as for instance in 'Paessaggio con pellegrino in preghiera' (p. 52), that Canaletto concentrates the light of the picture on the elements that have caught his fancy. This is also shown in the 'Carro sul ponte' where he brings the image right to the foreground by cutting a part from a larger plate, so that it almost stands out from the reconstructed perspective frame; it is likely that some more plates of his etchings had been intentionally cut by Canaletto (Ragghianti). Indeed, he probably developed his aesthetic feeling when he was working on his etchings. This is shown by the fact that he cut the plates and also by comparing the Berlin drawing 'Case rustiche e terrazza' (p. 77) and the etching that he produced by reducing the view to the terrace only, which thus limits the line of vision. It is true that in the drawing he already shows the tendency to a sensitive and light touch which was to become even thinner in the following years and yet still shows the artist's acute awareness, as in the other Berlin drawing, 'Case a destra di S. Basso' (p. 79), where the stalls of the stationer and the chemist are seen with a keen eye; and in 'Cantori nella basilica' (p. 81), which bears the proud inscription 'I, Zuane Antonio da Canal, did this drawing in 1766, at the age of 68, without spectacles'; this is all a play of liquid shadows

HOUSES ON THE RIGHT SIDE OF ST. BASSO
After 1755, pen and brown ink with little red chalk, 17 x 12
in. Berlin, Kupferstichkabinett

among the well-defined figures and objects and a perfect example of the bright and iridescent paintings of his later years. But Canaletto had also been influenced by his stay in England and by the example of Jacopo Amigoni, who had himself been to England. Canaletto went to England at least twice; the first time from May 1746 to Autumn 1750: and he went again after eight months to stay from 1751 to 1753. However, it is almost certain that he went again at least on another occasion because we have pictures dated 1754 'in London', and in 1755 Canaletto alludes in a drawing to a picture also painted in London.

We are not surprised at the stupendous view of 'London and the Thames from Richmond' (p. 62) belonging to the collection of the Duke of Richmond, which Canaletto painted soon after his arrival in London, with the open river in a huge landscape that goes as far as St. Paul's Cathedral, when we remember the pictures painted in Venice a few years earlier in a similar style.

It is certain that Canaletto, as soon as he arrived in England, when he looked at the Thames, still had in his mind the vision of the Basin of St. Mark; both views were enlarged as much as possible by his imagination till they reached an almost bound-less breadth. In the colours we find a new clarity and fresh-ness, probably the result of Canaletto's acquaintance, in 1746, with the English landscape in the ideal colours and atmosphere of Spring. In fact, in the view of the park of Warwick Castle (p. 61), drawn with a limited number of light strokes of the brush, the details of the terrace in the foreground are shown in an enchanting translucent atmosphere in delicate pastel shades of blue and pink.

Obviously this was different from his style of a few years earlier; these details, for instance, are unlike those of the 'Festa di S. Rocco' (p. 36), depicted in their full size in bright

CHOIR IN THE BASILICA OF ST. MARK
1766, pen and ink with brown wash, 14 x 11 in. Hamburg,
Kunsthalle

colours that reach the maximum chromatic vibration and refraction.

His clients, apparently, did not like this simplification of Canaletto's style in his English works. Vertue tells us that a rumour went around London at the time that the man who had landed in England was not really Canaletto, the painter of the great Venetian views imported into London by Smith. In fact Canaletto took the trouble to deny this rumour by advertising in the English papers in 1749 that anybody could visit him in his house in Silver Street to see the view 'St. James Park', which is probably the picture now belonging to the Count of Malmesbury. However, the rumour probably started on account of the change in Canaletto's style and the 'crisis' he went through.

Light had been always the most important means of expression of Canaletto's imagination all through his artistic career, at first in the contrasting chiaroscuro effects as a dramatic element, later as an optical medium to represent his figures with a sharp and clearly defined outline. This brilliance is now condensed into a few short strokes of the brush that make the figures and the objects stand out to the surface, establishing a direct contact between the realities represented and the viewer. An example of this is the delightful picture of the 'Park of Badminton House' (p. 67), with the deep yellow circular terrace in the foreground and, in the distance, the green fields and the trees under the huge sky that covers the whole width of the picture, giving a feeling of space and poetry; the details are un-forgettable like the amusing scene with the dogs and the horses in the park, and seem to come forward towards the viewer, The dazzling clearness of his vision seems to reach its peak in these first years of Canaletto in England; as in the view 'London through an Arch of Westminster Bridge' (p. 70), which is surprisingly modern. In the foreground is the arch of the bridge silhouetted against the light, and in the background, on the other side, the stones of the building are caught in their bare, sharp beauty. And 'Westminster Bridge' in the Bodkin Collection in London (p. 65) gives him the opportunity to catch the colourful life on the river, which he interprets in a cold and translucent atmosphere through a myriad of bright details in a wide range of sparkling colours.

Canaletto painted the Thames over and over again. This is not suprising since, apart from reminding him of his native Venice, he loved the Thames which represented to him every moment of the history and civilization of England to which he had become so deeply attached. The Thames inspired him with grandiose views, like those 'from Somerset House', the two pictures of the Royal Collection in Windsor, and the other two similar pictures which were bought in 1752 in London by Ferdinando Filippo of Lobkovicz and are now in the Nelahozeves Castle (p. 64) and in the National Gallery in Prague (p. 68). These show a huge boundless expanse of water and sky, interrupted by the narrow strip of the vividly descriptive view of the city. This skill of representing real details in an extremely spacious view achieves perfection around 1750, as in the splendid 'View of Whitehall', (p. 69), which Canaletto intended to bring with him to Venice when he returned from England and which he later sold to Mr. Crewe.

One cannot say with truth that Canaletto, in his English period, had no feeling for a picturesque effect nor that his reaction to the views was less emotional; that this is not the case is proved by the picturesque 'Warwick Castle' (p. 63), where the delightful details in the park of the castle of the Renaissance period remind us of the vivacious scenes in the villas along the Brenta riviera; there is also 'Alnwick Castle' where under a bright sky, crossed by a few pink clouds, the ancient walls of the mediaeval manor are set in the delightful green fields crowded with figures that can be compared to those of Zuccarelli (in England between 1752 and 1762); and by 'View of Eton with Chapel', in the National Gallery (p. 66), which includes the Thames and a charming part of the English countryside. How much Canaletto appreciated the picturesque quality of the English countryside and how much he was inspired by it is shown by the masterpiece 'Walton Bridge' (p. 71), in the Dulwich Gallery. In the Autumn sunset the neat architecture of the picturesque bridge is shown against a cloudy colourful sky, whilst there is peace and serenity in the beautiful open country. There is a deep feeling for Nature, a complete and total conformity to atmospherical changes and an intense and yet controlled abandonment that anticipates the romantic impressions of Constable's early works.

We know little about Canaletto after he came back from England. He certainly was not very successful in Venice in his later years. The Painters' Academy had been in existence since 1755; but when in 1763 he was recommended for a Fellowship, this was refused to him and it was instead granted to Pavona and Gradizzi. A few months later he did become a Fellow of the Academy, but there were some votes against it. For the occasion of his admission he painted in 1765 'Portico in prospettiva' (p. 72); this is his only picture kept in the Venetian Galleries. Although here he had to subdue his style to comply with the Academy's regulations, there are traces of his great art in the light and translucent touches, especially in the details, and also in the fascinating light. Without doubt the last works he painted for 'pleasure' are better: 'Piazza di S. Marco dal Caffè Florian' and 'dal Portico accanto a S. Geminiano'; especially the view from the Florian, with the unforgettable gentleman wearing a red coat and the stylized rays of light on the Doges' Palace. In these last years, when he painted the crowd scenes of the 'festivities' that were later engraved by Brustolon, his strokes, almost grotesquely thick, remind us of Domenico Tiepolo's bitter poetic feeling.

He died in Venice, when he was 71, on the 20th April 1766 in his house in S. Lio. Only twenty years after his death the Academic College, represented by Francesco Guardi, was called upon to decide the authenticity of very many pictures that were appearing on the market with Antonio Canal's signature. The counterfeits, the imitations, the copies, started to circulate probably when he was still alive and everybody knows how much they harmed Canaletto's reputation. Apart from followers and admirers who were not devoid of some talent, like the English Samuel Scott and the Italian Roberti, he had only two genuine interpreters of his vision, who were capable of recreating it with a spontaneous and true poetry: Francesco Guardi and Bernardo Bellotto.

In the nineteenth century we have had a revaluation of his art, although it was mainly academic, from Constable and Corot. And later he had a passionate admirer of the absolute value of his light in Manet.

LIST OF ILLUSTRATIONS